J 551.21 JEN
Jennings, Terry J.
Violent volcanoes

DATE DUE

Amazing Planet Earth

VIOLENT VOLCANOES

TERRY JENNINGS

A+

Smart Apple Media

Smart Apple Media
P.O. Box 3263
Mankato, MN 56002

Printed in the United States of America

Library of Congress Cataloging-in-Publication Data

Jennings, Terry J.
  Violent volcanoes / Terry Jennings.
     p. cm. -- (Amazing planet earth)
  Includes index.
  ISBN 978-1-59920-374-4 (hardcover)
  1. Volcanoes--Juvenile literature. I. Title.
  QE521.3.J45 2010
  551.21--dc22
                        2008055499

Created by Q2AMedia
Book Editor: Michael Downey
Art Director: Rahul Dhiman
Designer: Ranjan Singh
Picture Researcher: Shreya Sharma
Line Artist: Sibi N. Devasia
Coloring Artist: Mahender Kumar

Picture credits
t=top b=bottom c=center l=left r=right
Cover Images:Julien Grondin/ Shutterstock.
Back cover Image: Julien Grondin/ Shutterstock.

Insides: Julien Grondin/ Shutterstock: Title Page, Seiden Allan/ Pacific Stock/ Photolibrary: 4, Supri Supri/ Reuters Pictures: 5t, Donald A. Swanson/ USGS Photograph: 6b, Peter Lipman/ USGS Photograph: 6-7, Peter Lipman/ USGS Photograph: 8t, Dan Dzurisin/ USGS Photograph: 8b, Julien Grondin/ Shutterstock: 10b, The Natural History Museum/ Alamy: 11t, Russ Bishop/ Alamy: 12-13, J.D. Griggs/ USGS Photograph: 13t, Enote/ Shutterstock: 15, K. Segerstrom/ US. Geological Survey: 16, US. Geological Survey: 17b, Jesús Eloy Ramos Lara/ Dreamstime: 17t, Gregory Primo Photography/ Photographers Direct: 19t, National Geophysical Data Center: 18-19, Jacques Langevin/ Corbis Sygma: 20b, Wessel du Plooy/ Shutterstock: 21t, Rick Hoblitt/ US. Geological Survey: 23t, US. Geological Survey: 24, US. Geological Survey: 25, Peterm/ 123rf: 26, Zuki/ Istockphoto: 27, Peder Digre/ Shutterstock: 29, Enote/ Shutterstock: 31

Q2AMedia Art Bank: 9, 10, 14, 22, 28.

987654321

Contents

Violent Volcanoes

The world's loudest noise was made not by an atomic bomb, but by a volcano. In 1883, there was a volcanic eruption on the uninhabited Indonesian island of Krakatoa. The eruption was so loud, that people 3,100 miles (5,000 km) away in Australia heard the explosion. During the eruption, the land around Krakatoa shook so violently that nine gigantic ocean waves, or **tsunamis**, were formed. Huge, dark ash clouds also appeared. These clouds circled Earth for many years, blocking out the Sun's warmth and lowering temperatures on Earth's surface.

- **Red-hot lava streams run down the sides of Kilauea, a volcano on the island of Hawaii. Kilauea has been erupting since 1983.**

Liquid Rock

Although volcanoes have differently shaped **cones**, all were formed from hot liquid rock from deep inside Earth. Scientists believe that there are 1,511 **active volcanoes** on land, and many more that are no longer active. Some volcanoes **erupt** violently; others are more quiet.

Heat and Gases

Volcanoes play a vital part in forming islands, mountains, and valleys. They also allow unwanted heat and gases to escape from Earth. Valuable rocks and minerals are also produced from **lava** and other volcanic material.

● Krakatoa, in Indonesia, is still very active. The volcano is seen here erupting in 2001.

DATA FILE

- There are many active volcanoes on the floor of Earth's oceans.

- Most of Earth's active volcanoes are found around the Pacific Ocean.

- The old township of Rabaul in Papua New Guinea, which was built inside a volcano, was destroyed in 1994 by ash from a volcanic eruption.

- About 600 million people live close to active volcanoes.

- Millions of people farm the fertile soils that form from volcanic ash.

- The most deadly volcanic eruption was Indonesia's Mount Tambora, in 1815. This eruption resulted in 92,000 deaths.

Mount St. Helens

Until May 1980, Mount St. Helens stood 9,680 feet (2,950 m) high in the Cascade Range in the northwest United States. The land around it, a national park, was popular with nature lovers and sightseers. The peak of the mountain was covered with snow.

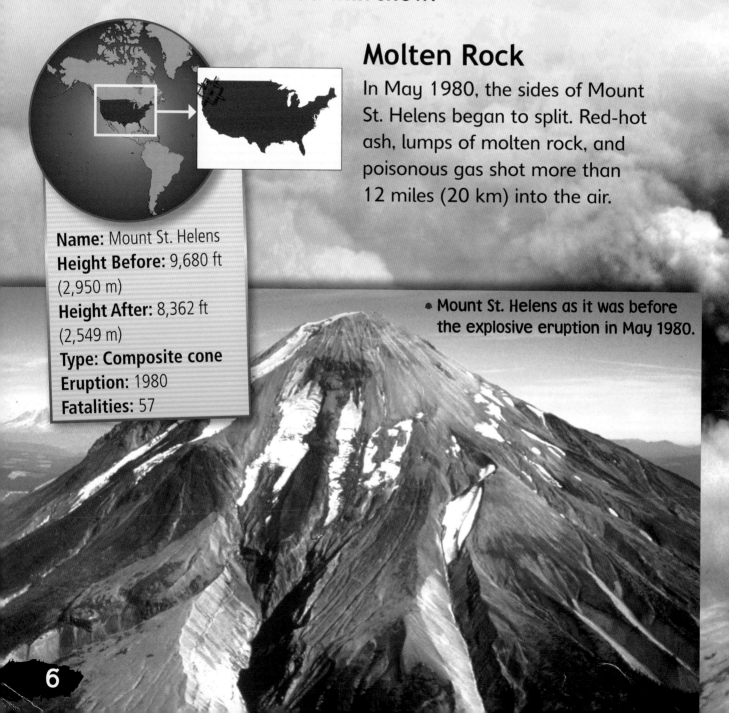

Molten Rock

In May 1980, the sides of Mount St. Helens began to split. Red-hot ash, lumps of molten rock, and poisonous gas shot more than 12 miles (20 km) into the air.

Name: Mount St. Helens
Height Before: 9,680 ft (2,950 m)
Height After: 8,362 ft (2,549 m)
Type: Composite cone
Eruption: 1980
Fatalities: 57

• Mount St. Helens as it was before the explosive eruption in May 1980.

Shattered Mountain

The eruption of Mount St. Helens gave off energy equivalent to thousands of nuclear bombs. The explosion, which shattered part of the top of the mountain, was heard in Vancouver, Canada, about 200 miles (320 km) away.

• **Mount St. Helens erupting in May 1980.**

News Flash

May 18, 1980

Mount St. Helens' volcano has erupted and killed 57 people. A nearby town has been evacuated. The volcano sent flames, ash, and black smoke up more than 12 miles (20 km). People 99 miles (160 km) away were thrown out of their beds by the force of the eruption.

Volcanic Cloud

Hot gas, ash, and rock from Mount St. Helens flattened over 10 million trees. A large chunk of the shattered mountain was swept into nearby Spirit Lake, and caused waves

• Trees were knocked down by the eruption of Mount St. Helens. The high temperatures boiled the sap in the trees.

656 feet (200 m) high. Two days later, the giant volcanic cloud had reached New York. Within two weeks, the cloud had traveled around the world.

• This car was buried in mud and lava 10 miles (16 km) away from Mount St. Helens.

Future Danger

In September 2003, a new dome of solidified lava began to form inside the **crater** of Mount St. Helens. Today, this dome is as tall as an 80-story building. In the future, it will totally fill the mountain and another huge eruption is likely.

The Moose Return

Many hundreds of moose died as a result of the eruption in 1980. However, their numbers are now increasing again in the region.

DATA FILE

- The earthquake that started the May 1980 explosion reached 5.1 on the Richter Scale.

- The huge blast area covered about 232 square miles (600 sq km).

- Millions of 200-year-old pine trees were flattened like matchsticks.

- Gas clouds moved at speeds of nearly 200 mph (320 km).

- Hot ash shot more than 7,000 feet (2,100 m) into the air.

- The temperature of the nearby Toutle River rose to 194°F (90°C).

BEFORE

- The peak of Mount St. Helens was nearly a perfect cone shape.

AFTER

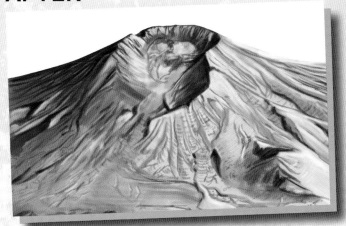

- The north side was blown apart and left a huge hole.

NOW

- The hole is slowly filling and the peak is growing back.

Why Do Volcanoes Erupt?

The inside of Earth is heating up all the time. Volcanoes are nature's way of letting heat escape and cooling Earth.

Hot Rocks

Earth is not a solid, unbroken mass. Instead, it is made up of several layers. We live on the thin outer layer of solid rock called the **crust**. This is about 18.5 miles (30 km) thick on land, but only 4–6 miles (6–10 km) thick under the oceans. Underneath the crust is a thick layer of hot rocks called the **mantle**. In places, the mantle has melted to form **magma**, which flows like sticky tar.

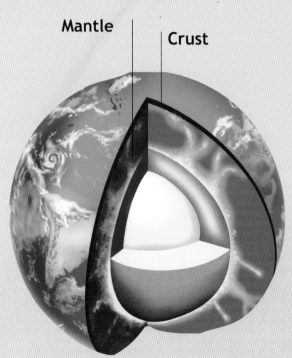

Mantle

Crust

• The layers of Earth.

• Red-hot magma erupts through Earth's crust and flows downhill.

Volcano

Crust

Plates

Mantle

Escaping magma

- Magma pushes against Earth's crust until it finds a weak spot.

Moving Plates

The crust is not a seamless layer around Earth. Instead, it is made up of smaller sections called **plates** that fit together like a jigsaw puzzle. The plates float on liquid magma that constantly pushes up against the plates. Wherever there is a weak spot, the magma rises toward the surface, creating a volcano. Usually, this is a place close to where two plates meet.

DATA FILE

- There are seven major plates and many minor plates.

- Plates move from a fraction of an inch to about 5 inches (13 cm) a year.

- Most volcanoes and earthquakes occur where plates meet.

- Plates are about 62 miles (100 km) thick.

- Plates can push into each other, pull away from each other, slide by each other, or one plate can slide over the top of another.

- A plate moving at 2 inches (5 cm) a year will travel about 31 miles (50 km) in a million years.

Mauna Loa

Some of the world's most beautiful islands were made by volcanoes. This is true of the Hawaiian Islands in the Pacific Ocean. These islands are actually the tips of undersea mountains that were formed by volcanoes.

● Mauna Loa erupting in 1984.

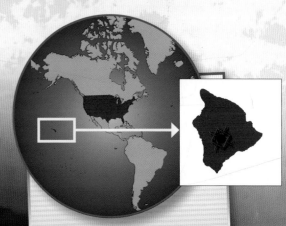

Name: Mauna Loa
Location: Hawaii
Height: 13,680 ft (4,170 m)
Type: Shield cone
Eruption: 1984
Fatalities: None

Largest Volcano

There are several volcanoes on the island of Hawaii. One of them, Mauna Loa, is the world's largest active volcano. It last erupted in 1984. When Mauna Loa erupts, it produces hot, runny lava that flows long distances before it cools and hardens. This is why the volcano has gently sloping sides and, at 62 miles (100 km) across, is extremely wide. At its top, or summit, Mauna Loa has a huge oval crater that is the world's second largest crater. Mauna Loa, and its neighboring Kilauea volcano, are visited by many tourists each year. Visitors can approach the rim of the volcanoes and look directly down into their craters.

Time to Escape

Mauna Loa is a fairly quiet volcano. Although the lava it produces is destructive and can do immense damage to crops and livestock, it moves slowly. The number of human lives this volcano has claimed is low, as people usually have time to pack their possessions and leave the area.

Inside a Volcano

Most volcanoes occur where Earth's plates crash together or break apart. Two-thirds of the world's active volcanoes are found around the edge of the Pacific Ocean, where several plates meet.

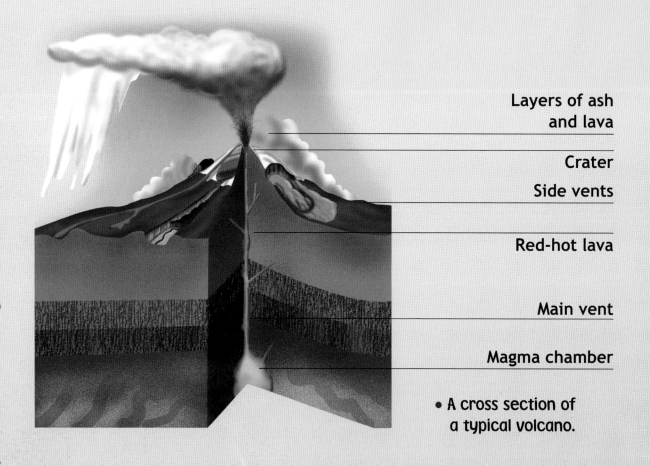

Layers of ash and lava

Crater

Side vents

Red-hot lava

Main vent

Magma chamber

• A cross section of a typical volcano.

Magma and Lava

Where Earth's crust is thin, magma rises and forms large underground pools, called **magma reservoirs**.

As the magma collects, it presses against the surrounding rock. When it finds a weak spot, the magma forces its way up a **vent** and bursts to the surface forming a volcano.

Volcanic Bombs

Although magma reaches the surface through a volcano's main crater, other openings can appear in the sides of a volcano. When blasted high into the air, lava may harden into huge lumps of rock called volcanic bombs.

Hot-Spot Volcanoes

Not all volcanoes are found near the edges of Earth's plates. The Hawaiian Islands, for example, were made by volcanoes and are about 2,000 miles (3,200 km) from the nearest plate edges. Scientists believe that rising magma can push a hole in a weak part of Earth's crust, known as a hot spot, to form a volcano.

• Tanzania's Mount Kilimanjaro is one of the world's largest inactive volcanoes.

DATA FILE

- Stromboli, a volcano off the coast of Italy, has been active since records began more than 2,500 years ago. It erupts about once every 20 minutes.

- More than 80 percent of Earth's surface was produced by volcanoes. Gases from volcanoes formed Earth's atmosphere.

- Huge lightning flashes may be seen during volcanic eruptions. It is believed that the millions of hot particles rubbing together produce giant sparks.

- In 1963, fishermen off the coast of Iceland watched a mound of black, steaming rock slowly rise up from the sea. Over the years, a new volcanic island, now called Surtsey, formed at this spot.

Paricutin

Paricutin is famous for giving scientists an incredible opportunity. For the first time, it was possible to study a volcano from the time it was formed until it died.

Name: Paricutin
Location: Southwestern Mexico
Height: 9,215 ft (2,809 m)
Type: Cinder cone
Eruption: 1943–1952
Fatalities: 3

New Volcano

In February 1943, a crack 20 inches (50 cm) deep opened in a cornfield near Paricutin, Mexico. The ground rose by 6.5 feet (2 m), and a thick cloud of smoke and ashes shot upward. A few hours later, red-hot rocks were hurled into the air. A new volcano was forming. By the same time the next day, the cornfield was covered by a cone of ashes 164 feet (50 m) high. Seven days later, the cone of ashes was 492 feet (150 m) high.

- The eruption of Paricutin began in 1943 and ended in 1952.

- Only the church towers are visible above the lava that buried Paricutin.

Crater Rim

After a year, the cone was 1,102 feet (336 m) high. The new cinder cone volcano erupted for another 8 years, with about one billion tons of lava. In February 1952, it suddenly stopped. By then, the crater rim stood 1,345 feet (410 m) above the remains of the cornfield.

- Scientists collect samples from Paricutin's cinder cone.

Nevado del Ruiz

Mud, as well as hot volcanic ash and lava, can be fatal. Many people died from the deadly mudflows that resulted when Colombia's snowcapped volcano, Nevado del Ruiz, erupted.

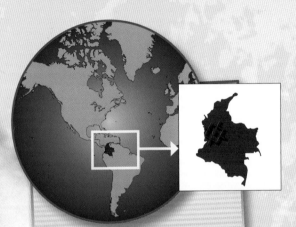

Name: Nevado del Ruiz
Location: Central Colombia
Height: 17,457 ft (5,321 m)
Type: Composite cone
Eruption: 1985
Fatalities: 23,000

Warning Ignored

Local people called Nevado del Ruiz the Sleeping Lion because it had been inactive, or a **dormant volcano**, for nearly 150 years. In November 1984, however, the volcano began puffing steam and ash. Scientists were worried and warned that a disaster was possible. They recommended that evacuation plans be made. The government took little notice of the warning as the volcano was a long way from any towns or villages.

• The main active crater of Nevado del Ruiz volcano.

• Although Nevado del Ruiz is near the equator, its summit is extremely high and permanently covered in snow.

Black Mud

In the afternoon of November 13, 1985, there was a small eruption as Nevado del Ruiz began to eject ash. The main eruption began in the evening. In about 3 hours, 26 millon cubic yards (20 million cubic meters) of hot ashes and rocks poured out of the vent. This covered the volcano's snow cap as well as the small glacier that ran down one side. Beneath the blanket of hot ashes and rocks, the snow and ice around the summit of Nevado del Ruiz quickly melted. This caused a torrent of slimy, black mud to pour down a river valley on the northern slopes of the volcano.

Lethal Lahars

Waves of the mudflows, up to 131 feet (40 m) deep, raced down the sides of the volcano at speeds of 31 miles (50 km) per hour or more. Boulders, trees, bridges, and people in the path of the mudflows were swept away or buried. The mudflows, called **lahars**, headed toward the small town of Armero, some 46 miles (74 km) away. Picking up water and mud from the river valleys, the deadly lahars grew in size as they moved away from the volcano.

- The town of Armero was buried in mud that was produced when hot ash mixed with water from melting ice and snow.

Armero Destroyed

It took only two-and-one-half hours for the mudflows to reach Armero. A warning had been sent out, but it did not reach the people in time. Armero was destroyed. Only 100 of its 5,000 houses remained intact. Amazingly, the cemetery survived unscathed. Altogether, the lahars killed 23,000 people, which included 90 percent of the population of Armero. There were thousands of deaths in surrounding villages, and many pets and farm animals died.

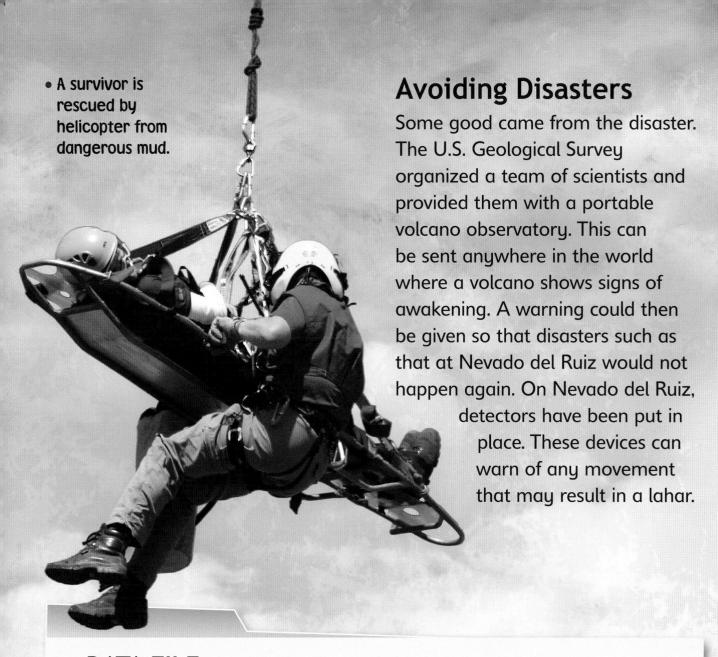

● A survivor is rescued by helicopter from dangerous mud.

Avoiding Disasters

Some good came from the disaster. The U.S. Geological Survey organized a team of scientists and provided them with a portable volcano observatory. This can be sent anywhere in the world where a volcano shows signs of awakening. A warning could then be given so that disasters such as that at Nevado del Ruiz would not happen again. On Nevado del Ruiz, detectors have been put in place. These devices can warn of any movement that may result in a lahar.

DATA FILE

- The Nevado del Ruiz tragedy marked the second worst volcanic disaster of the twentieth century.

- As well as 23,000 human deaths, about 15,000 animals died.

- Armero had been built on the top of old mudflows from the volcano.

- In Armero, the mud destroyed 2

hospitals, 50 schools, 58 factories, and 343 shops and offices.

- About 60 percent of the area's farm animals and 30 percent of the rice crop were destroyed.

- Many people who only had minor cuts died when their wounds became infected by the dirty mud.

Volcano Shapes

The hill, or mountain, around the vent of a volcano is called a cone. The three main types of cone are the cinder cone, shield cone, and composite cone.

Cinder Cone

When volcanoes erupt with great violence, burning gases, hot ash, and **cinders** are forced high into the sky. The eruption builds up a steep cone of ashes and cinders around the volcano's vent. This results in a cinder cone volcano, such as Paricutin in Mexico.

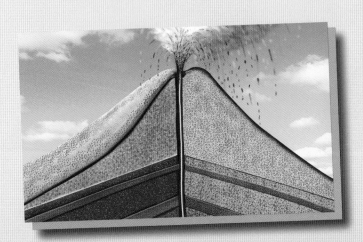

Shield Cone

When lava is runny, it spreads out around the crater before hardening. The lava forms a gently sloping volcano, like a shield lying on the ground. This is why a volcano such as Mauna Loa is called a shield cone.

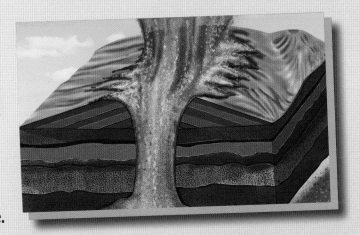

Composite Cone

If a volcano erupts quietly and then violently, a tall, composite cone is produced. This is made up of layers of different materials. Mount St. Helens in the United States is a composite cone.

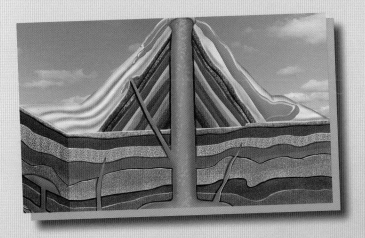

• Mount Pinatubo in the Philippines, a composite cone volcano, erupted in 1991 with tremendous force. Thousands of buildings were destroyed.

Active, Extinct, and Dormant Volcanoes

Although a few volcanoes erupt all the time, most only erupt now and then. A volcano that erupts is called active. Volcanoes, such as Mount Kilimanjaro in Tanzania and Mount Shasta in the United States, have not erupted for thousands of years and are said to be **extinct volcanoes**. Other volcanoes are dormant, or sleeping. It is not always easy to tell whether a volcano is dormant or extinct. Scientists thought that Eldfell volcano on the island of Heimaey, near Iceland, was extinct. But 1973, it erupted violently and destroyed 300 buildings.

DATA FILE

- Argentina's Aconcagua is the highest extinct volcano. It is 22,835 feet (6,960 m) high.

- Ecuador's Cotopaxi is one of the tallest active volcanoes. This composite cone is 19,390 feet (5,911 m) high.

- The world's largest dormant volcano is Haleakala on Maui, one of Hawaii's islands. It is 10,000 feet (3,048 m) high.

- At 19,340 feet (5,895 m), Tanzania's extinct volcano Mount Kilimanjaro is the highest free-standing mountain in the world.

- About 60 percent of the world's volcanoes have composite cones.

Lake Nyos

Lake Nyos is perched high on a mountain in Cameroon, West Africa. Unlike most other lakes, Lake Nyos fills the crater of a volcano that last erupted several centuries ago.

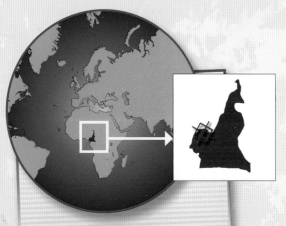

Name: Lake Nyos
Location: Northwestern Cameroon, West Africa
Height: 9,879 ft (3,011 m)
Type: Crater lake
Eruption: 1986
Fatalities: 1,700

Danger in the Depths

The waters of Lake Nyos hide a deadly secret. Deep below, carbon dioxide slowly bubbles out from tiny holes in blocked volcanic vents at the bottom of the lake. The surface of the lake is warmed by the hot sun. But 656 feet (200 m) down, the water is cold and thick with the gas.

• Under the surface of Lake Nyos, carbon dioxide seeps into its cold waters.

Deadly Cloud

On the evening of August 21, 1986, carbon dioxide gas at the bottom of Lake Nyos suddenly gushed upward and formed a huge cloud above the surface of the lake. As carbon dioxide is heavier than other gases in the air, the cloud hugged the ground and rushed down to the villages below, reaching speeds of 31 miles (50 km) per hour. In the villages, it put out cooking fires and people suffocated in their beds. In the village of Subum, 6 miles (10 km) from the lake, patients on the top floor of the hospital were unharmed, while those downstairs suffocated. The gas cloud killed 1,700 people, 6,000 cattle, and countless birds and mammals.

- These cows were just of a few of the thousands of domestic animals killed by the deadly clouds of gas from Lake Nyos.

Safety Pipes

Scientists have now placed plastic pipes in Lake Nyos to circulate its water. This allows small amounts of carbon dioxide gas to bubble out and escape safely into the air.

Yellowstone Park

Situated in the border areas of Wyoming, Montana, and Idaho, Yellowstone National Park is famous for the hundreds of **geysers**, **hot springs**, and bubbling **mudpots** found within its boundaries.

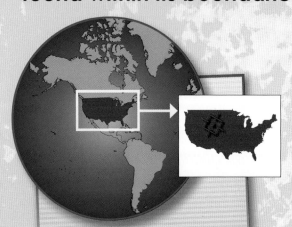

Name: Old Faithful
Location: Yellowstone National Park, Wyoming
Height: Column of water 98–180 ft (30–55 m) high
Type: Geysers
Eruption: About every 66 to 80 minutes

Giant Caldera

Almost all of Yellowstone National Park lies in a huge basin called a **caldera**. This was formed about 600,000 years ago when a gigantic ancient volcano erupted and then collapsed. The magma chamber that formed the original volcano is still present, about 4 miles (6 km) below the surface. Underneath Yellowstone's caldera is a hot spot that slowly moves at the rate of about 1.4 inches (3.5 cm) per year.

• Terraces at Mammoth Hot Springs in Yellowstone Park. These form when hot water streams down a slope, evaporates, and leaves behind dissolved chemicals that harden.

Steaming Fumaroles

Above the Yellowstone magma chamber, there are over 300 geysers. This is more than anywhere else in the world. The most famous geyser is Old Faithful. There are also about 10,000 hot springs, mudpots, and steaming **fumaroles**. Like Old Faithful, they are heated by the magma chamber.

Old Faithful

On average, Old Faithful erupts every 66 to 80 minutes. Ten minutes before it erupts, this geyser bubbles and splutters. It then shoots up a column of steam and boiling water between 100–180 feet (30–55 m) into the air.

- Old Faithful Geyser in Wyoming has been erupting almost every hour for hundreds of years.

DATA FILE

- When Old Faithful erupts, 11,890 gallons (45,000 L) of hot water and steam are discharged.

- The average height of one eruption is 144 feet (44 m).

- Each eruption lasts between 1.5 and 5 minutes.

- The water temperature at 656 feet (200 m) below the surface is 392°F (200°C).

- Another geyser in Yellowstone Park, called Steamboat, produces the world's highest spurt of water and steam. It can reach 400 feet (200 m).

Lakes, Geysers, and Hot Springs

Lakes, known as crater lakes, can form in volcanic craters. In some areas, such as Yellowstone National Park, geysers, hot springs, mudpots, and fumaroles heated by hot rocks underground are also found.

Crater Lakes

Lake Nyos was formed in the crater of a volcano. High in the mountains of Oregon, there is another circular lake nearly 2,000 feet (600 m) deep. Known as Crater Lake, it was formed when the sides of the volcano collapsed inward after a series of eruptions. Rainwater then filled the large cavity known as a caldera.

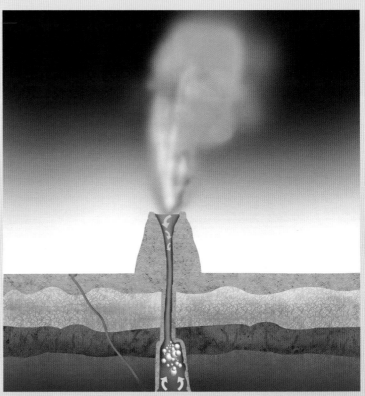
• How a geyser is formed.

Bubbling Mudpots

Geysers are formed when water from the surface seeps down, collects underground, and is heated by the hot rocks. A jet of steam and boiling water then shoots high into the air with great force. When enough water has seeped back into the ground, the process is repeated. Sulfuric acid, sometimes found near a geyser, dissolves the surrounding rock and produces a slimy, bubbling mudpot.

Converting Steam

As well as being popular tourist attractions, geysers and hot springs have other uses. In Iceland, for example, water from hot springs is used to heat homes, swimming pools, and greenhouses. In other countries, such as Italy, Mexico, and New Zealand, water from hot springs is piped to power stations to be turned into steam. The steam turns the turbines that generate electricity.

- Crater Lake is the second deepest lake in the United States. It occupies a crater that was formed by a series of overlapping volcanoes.

DATA FILE

- The Ngorongo Crater, in Tanzania, is covered with dry, grassy plains that are home to more than 30,000 wild animals.

- In 1864, a hotel in Oregon began to heat rooms using energy from underground hot springs.

- In Iceland, tropical fruits such as bananas and pineapples are grown in greenhouses heated by hot water from geysers.

- The first **geothermal power** station opened in Italy in 1911.

- Geothermal power is now used in more than 20 countries.

Glossary

active volcano a volcano that erupts from time to time

caldera a huge, bowl-shaped cavity formed when a volcano collapses into its empty magma chamber after it has erupted

cinders small pieces of partly burned material

cinder cone a volcano with a steep cone of ashes and cinders; cinder cone volcanoes usually erupt with great violence

composite cone a tall, cone-shaped volcano built up by many eruptions; it is made of layers of lava and layers of ashes and cinders

cone the hill or mountain formed by a volcano

crater the funnel-shaped hole at the top of a volcano

crust Earth's outer layer of rock on which we live

dormant volcano a volcano that is resting or inactive, not erupting

erupt magma is forced out of a weak spot in Earth's crust forming a volcano

extinct volcano a volcano that is no longer active

fumarole a small opening in the ground through which hot gases can escape from deep inside Earth

geothermal power the energy produced using the steam from water that is heated by the red-hot rocks beneath the surface of Earth

geyser a hot spring that throws a jet of hot water and steam into the air from time to time

hot spring a stream of hot water coming from the ground

lahar a muddy flow of water mixed with ash and other material from an erupting volcano; a lahar is often called a mudflow

lava the molten rock that comes out of a volcano

magma the hot molten, or liquid, rock formed in Earth's mantle just below the crust

magma reservoir a large pool of magma beneath the surface of Earth

mantle   the layer of rock below Earth's crust and above the core; the mantle is thought to be so hot that some of the rocks have melted and are a sticky liquid

mudpot   a pool of hot, bubbling mud that is usually white or gray in color

plates   the sections of Earth's crust; the slow, steady movements of the plates cause changes in Earth's surface

shield cone a gently sloping volcano, formed by liquid lava that has spread out around the crater of the volcano

tsunami   a large sea wave, usually caused by an earthquake on the sea bed

vent   the opening in a volcano from which lava, gases, ashes, and cinders erupt

Index

Web Sites

www.fema.gov/kids/volcano.htm
This site offers basic information about volcanoes.

www.learner.org/interactives/volcanoes/entry.html
This site provides information on how we can predict volcanic eruptions and how best to deal with them.

http://education.usgs.gov/common/primary.htm#volcanoes
A site containing educational resources for teachers of young children. The site includes live views of volcanoes around the world.